For all our little sisters in our faith families:
you are good and necessary.

With love and affection,
Jen & Zoe

"As the parents of two daughters, we've always wanted to share with them the wonderful way God made them and fashioned them in his image. We're thankful to see a mother and daughter celebrate together God's good design for women in this new children's book. *It's Good to Be a Girl* is a wonderful way to communicate to our daughters their beauty and worth in God's sight."

MICHAEL & MELISSA KRUGER, RTS CHARLOTTE & TGC

"Being a girl is one of God's greatest gifts, and this winsome and delightful book showcases God's good design for women throughout Scripture. Daughters and granddaughters will see with fresh eyes God's purposeful plan to use women in vital roles in his plan of redemption, inviting each young reader to walk closely with Jesus and be used by him."

AMY GANNETT, TINY THEOLOGIANS

"A beautifully illustrated story to share with your daughter, packed with positivity and freedom, with the message that it's good to be who God made us to be."

AMY SMITH, FAITH IN KIDS

"This book is refreshing! Sadly, girls in our culture are bombarded with misogynistic messages, even from a young age. In seeking to combat this, many authors do so in ways that only encourage self-centeredness and pride. But Jen and Zoe Oshman have written a wonderful book that helps girls understand the true source of their dignity and value—being created in God's image and being recreated through the gospel. I can't wait to read this with our daughter!"

SHAI LINNE, RAPPER & AUTHOR

It's Good to Be a Girl
© Jen Oshman and Zoe Oshman 2024

Illustrated by Hsulynn Pang | Design & Art Direction by André Parker

Published in association with the literary agency of Wolgemuth & Wilson

"The Good Book For Children" is an imprint of The Good Book Company Ltd
North America: thegoodbook.com UK: thegoodbook.co.uk Australia: thegoodbook.com.au New Zealand: thegoodbook.co.nz India: thegoodbook.co.in

ISBN: 9781784989804 | JOB-007406 | Printed in India

thegoodbook
for children

Written by Jen and Zoe Oshman
Illustrated by Hsulynn Pang

It's Good to Be a Girl

A Celebration of All That God
Made You to Be

Do you know something?
    I *love* having a little girl.
Do you know why?
    Because girls are special and needed!

What do you mean?

Let me show you...

Way back when God created Adam, the very first man, he already had plans to create Eve, the very first woman.

God knew that it was not good for man
to be alone. Adam needed a helper—
and that was Eve.

God chose to make me who I am,
    A needed part of God's good plan.
Let's thank our God, rejoice and twirl,
    Because it's good to be a girl!

You know who else the Bible says is a helper?
God! He made Eve to be like him. In fact, God
made both boys and girls in his image. He made
us to love and serve others just like he does.

God is a helper. Eve is a helper.
And all girls can be helpers!

Helpers can defend and
rescue people in harm's way.

Helpers can give life
and protect life.

Helpers are brave and
helpers make peace.

Helpers can
lift those who
are down.

Eve was just the first of many helpers God made!

Miriam watched over her brother when he was in danger.

Deborah ruled her people with fairness.

Exodus 2:1-10

Judges 4:4-5

Abigail made peace
when there could
have been a big fight.

1 Samuel 25:14-35

And Esther stood
up against Israel's
enemies.

Esther 7:1-6

They were all doing
the kinds of things that
God does.

We saved and served and helped and loved,
Just like our God in heaven above.
Let's thank our God, rejoice and twirl,
Because it's good to be a girl!

So... how can I be like those girls in the Bible?

All you need to do is trust in Jesus!

How do I do that?

Well, when you spend time with Jesus, by spending time with his Word, his Spirit, and his people, he will grow you and change you. As you get to know him better, you will trust him more and more! He will show you just how to love him and others.

Just like he helped Mary and Martha. They were sisters who listened to Jesus and loved him.

Luke 10:38-39

Acts 16:14-15

Or like Lydia. She was a businesswoman who used her home to help her church.

Romans 16:3-4

Or like Priscilla. She and her husband, Aquila, risked their lives to share God's love.

Or like Eunice. She was a mom who passed on her faith in Jesus to her son Timothy.

2 Timothy 1:5

They couldn't have done it without Jesus!

With Jesus' help we knew the way—
He made us more like him each day!
Let's thank our God, rejoice and twirl,
Because it's good to be a girl!

You know, God chose
to make you exactly
who you are—
inside and out!

Really? Are you sure?

Yes! God made every girl unique—just the way he wants!

And he puts every girl right where she is, so she can love him and love others.

Like Harriet Tubman, who led hundreds of enslaved people to freedom.

1820 – 1913

1908 – 1997

And Esther Ahn Kim, who kept sharing God's love with others even when she was put in jail.

And Fanny Crosby, who wrote thousands of songs praising God.

1820 – 1915

And every girl who shows love and care for others in one hundred ordinary and unseen ways.

All of us are a special part of God's good plan!

God shapes our lives and helps us do
Whatever he has called us to.
Let's thank our God, rejoice and twirl,
Because it's good to be a girl!

And you know what?

Today God still helps us to love him and love others. He helps girls who are students and scientists, teachers and track stars, mommies and missionaries, doctors and dancers, woodworkers and wives, computer coders and cab drivers!

With Jesus' help, every girl can do anything God asks her to do!

Oh, how I want to be just like those girls!

You can be! And in some ways you already are.

God made you, and all girls, to be like him. As you grow and as you go, if you ask him, he will help you to love him and others in all that you do!

Let's thank our God, rejoice and twirl,
I'm very glad that I'm a girl!

Dear parents and caregivers,

As mother and daughter, we've had this conversation for over two decades now: what does it mean to be a girl? What's our purpose here? As we've searched the Scriptures, we've been overwhelmed by the goodness in God's design for Eve and all her daughters.

In Genesis 2:18 we see God make a "helper" fit for Adam. The word for "helper" in the original Hebrew language is *ezer*. It is used 21 times in the Old Testament, including 16 times as a description of God himself. *Ezer* is associated with shields, swords, triumph, rescue, comfort, and awe. What an amazing calling!

We want the girls in your life to know that God designed them to be good and necessary—and to understand all the possibilities God has for them.

As you have been called to care for and raise up little girls in the 21st century, perhaps you have felt burdened and even overwhelmed by gender and identity issues, which whirl around us. We certainly have. But here's what's true: God's Word is timeless, good, true, and beautiful. As our Creator and Savior, Jesus has only the very best in mind for you, and us, and every single girl in the world.

May we cling to God and his word, and may we renew our minds according to what he says. May this book help you, and the girls you love, to do just that.

It really is good to be a girl!

Jen and Zoe Oshman